Birth of a School

This book gives the account of how St. Joseph's R.C. High School came into being, and the considerable struggle involved. It may come as a surprise to many that Roman Catholic schools did not get built just because there was a need, as was the case with state schools. Education authorities had to be convinced, particularly in the case of secondary schools, that such schools should be included in a building programme, in view of the economic climate of the 1960s and 1970s, sometimes to the exclusion of one of their own schools. Such was the case with St. Joseph's R.C. High School, which was established at a revolutionary period in British education, the start of comprehensive schooling.

The mid 1960s saw the building of many large comprehensive schools. The desire of local Catholics to have their own comprehensive school was opposed at each point by the local education authority that wanted to build their own schools as a priority.

Eventually, in September 1967, St. Joseph's was established using Tredegar House and two R.C. Secondary Modern schools in the town, and Phase I of the new building was started in November 1968. The building of Phase II was also postponed and another struggle to get it into a building programme ensued. This Phase was not commenced until 1972, the final Phase III being completed in 1976.

The founding of St. Joseph's R.C. High School was unique in many respects, not least in that it was brought about mainly by the pressure and actions of parents who had to persuade Newport Local Education Authority, the Welsh Office and, initially, the Archdiocese, to commit funds needed to build the School.

J. ALAN SHEWRING

Joseph Alan Shewring was born in Newport and educated at St. Julian's High School. After leaving school he trained as a Chartered Accountant and qualified in 1959. He subsequently joined Notley and Pearson, the South Wales firm of Chartered Accountants, and became a partner in 1967. The firm eventually became Notley Pearson Shewring and he was Managing Partner for some 15 years until it merged in 2000.

He was a founder member of Family Care Housing Association (since renamed Charter Housing), which is a major provider of social housing in Newport and Monmouthshire, and was its first Treasurer.

Alan Shewring has been a school governor since 1967 both in the secondary and primary school sectors, and was a member of the Archdiocesan Education Commission for a number of years.

Birth
of a School

ST. JOSEPH'S R.C. HIGH SCHOOL
TREDEGAR PARK, NEWPORT, SOUTH WALES

J. ALAN SHEWRING

APECS PRESS △ CAERLEON

Published by
Apecs Press
Caerleon
Wales UK

ISBN 0 9548940 0 6

Printed in Wales by Gwasg Dinefwr Llandybie

In memory of Jane

CONTENTS

ACKNOWLEDGEMENTS

I am indebted to Sister Pauline for supplying information about the transition of St. Joseph's Convent High School to the Comprehensive School. It gave me the opportunity to renew our very good friendship which has extended over a period of nearly 50 years.

I must acknowledge, also, the advice and assistance given me by my good friend, Dr. Alun Isaac, whose knowledge and experience in publishing has been invaluable.

The support of Sue Jenkins, the present Head of the School, given unhesitatingly, and of the Chairman of Governors, Paul Bennett, is much appreciated.

The artistic skills of Alan Kethro and David Haylock in the School's Art Department have been significant in the production of the book's covers and the photographs.

Finally, the patience and typographical skills of my wife, Christine, have been indispensable.

FOREWORD

This book provides an account of how a group of dedicated parents, with great effort and persistence, enabled a Catholic comprehensive school to be opened and built. It illustrates how small groups with strong beliefs and values were able to influence and change the decisions of local and state education authorities.

Alan Shewring, one of that small band of parents, recounts how this was achieved, and how St. Joseph's R.C. High School was eventually born.

Great pride can be taken in how the School, then established, has developed since, and the successes many of its pupils have achieved in their chosen careers. But most importantly, that a comprehensive school came into being that had a Christian character and ethos.

This fascinating book will be of interest to parents, pupils, former pupils of the School, and those interested in Catholic education and may come as a surprise to many. When they see the magnificent new school building, which has replaced the original buildings, those achievements in the 1960s and 1970s will be brought into focus.

The Catholic community in Newport and the surrounding areas will be indebted to the author for this historical account of what happened locally in Catholic education some 40 years ago.

The author was a Foundation Governor of St. Joseph's R.C. High School from September 1967, when the first governing body was appointed, to January 1991. He was Chairman of Governors from 1973 to 1986 and 1988 to 1991.

Alan Shewring also wrote *Guidelines for Governors of Catholic Schools in Wales* for the Archdiocese of Cardiff and the Diocese of Menevia. (Published 1983).

S. M. Jenkins
Headteacher
St. Joseph's R.C. High School
April 1997 to Present

INTRODUCTION

The involvement of parents in the struggle to establish a Catholic high school for boys and girls in Newport came in 1964. At that time there were three Catholic secondary schools in Newport – St. Joseph's Convent High School for Girls at Tredegar House, Father Hill Secondary Modern School for Boys at Oswald Road (now the site of St. Michael's Primary School), and Holy Family Secondary Modern School for Girls at Emlyn Street (since demolished). There was no provision for Catholic boys who aspired to a grammar school education. Some of these travelled to St. Illtyd's R.C. High School in Cardiff, where there was a small intake of Newport boys, the remainder attending the two grammar schools in Newport – Newport High School or St. Julian's High School. Comprehensive schools were only just being established, the first being Duffryn High School which was built in the mid 1960s.

As far back as 1950 the need for a Catholic high school in Newport had been taken up with the Local Education Authority (LEA). In 1965, the LEA's agreement to the use of Newport High School (Queens Hill) to found a Catholic high school was revoked. Subsequently, the Archbishop of Cardiff, the Most Reverend Dr. John Murphy met representatives from the Ministry and the LEA who agreed to allow the proposed School to take the place of proposed extensions to St. Julian's High School on the building programme for 1966/67. This decision was also revoked.

Meanwhile, in 1964 a small group of Catholic parents, alarmed at the continuing delays, formed the Catholic Parents' and Electors' Association as a pressure group to get a Catholic high school estab-

1

lished. Great concern was felt by parents that progress on the project was too slow and was being delayed unnecessarily.

The Joint Managers and Governors of the Catholic Primary and Secondary Modern Schools had earlier set up a working group to explore how such a School could be established, motivated by Father Tom Lenane, who was then Parish Priest of St. Mary's, Stow Hill.

PARENTAL INFLUENCE

Catholic Parents' and Electors' Association (CPEA)

This Association was formed to give concerned parents an official identity and a representative body in their struggle to establish a Catholic high school in Newport for their children. After the formalities of adopting a constitution, enrolling members, electing a committee of members, and registering with the National Association had been accomplished, lines of communication were opened with the Joint Managers and Governors of the Newport Catholic Schools, and then with the Local Education Authority. At the first meeting on 28th January 1965 it was agreed that the Association should be on a district basis, i.e. Newport and Monmouthshire Branch, and that parish associations also should be formed.

The first officers of the district association were: Chairman – Leo Driscoll, Vice-chairman – Dr. John Savage, and Secretary – Michael Savage.

Leo Driscoll, a former Newport Councillor, was Correspondent Manager of the Joint Managers and Governors. Dr. John Savage was a local General Practitioner, and was to emigrate to Nova Scotia within a few years. He eventually entered politics and became Prime Minister of Nova Scotia. Michael Savage, his brother, was a Solicitor in practice in Newport.

During the next eighteen months, the officers changed, and St. Mary's Parish Branch of the Association took the lead in the effort to found the School. The officers of the St. Mary's Parish Branch were: Chairman – Alan Shewring, Vice-Chairman – Aubrey Hames, and Secretary – Tony Boyle.

Alan Shewring had attended St. Julian's High School, one of the two grammar schools in Newport, and had converted to Catholicism in 1956 after meeting his late wife, Jane. A Chartered Accountant by profession, he was a partner in the South Wales firm which eventually became Notley Pearson Shewring. Although not having had a Catholic education, like most of his fellow parents, he wanted the benefits of this for his children, all three of whom progressed to St. Joseph's.

Aubrey Hames was a well-known figure locally being a town councillor and a prominent member of the Labour Party Group in Newport. He held a senior management position with British Transport at Newport Docks, and later in Cardiff Docks. He had been a close second for the nomination to contest the parliamentary election for the Labour Party won by Roy Hughes who went on to represent Newport in the House of Commons for some 30 years. The view of many at that time was that Aubrey would have been a very effective Member of Parliament. He went on to give years of distinguished service on Newport Council, eventually being made an Alderman of the Borough and its Mayor in 1977/78. He and his wife, Mary, had four children, all of whom attended St. Joseph's in due course.

Tony Boyle hailed from Liverpool and it was his career development that brought him to Newport in the early 1960s. Educated at Stoneyhurst College and Cambridge University, from where he graduated in Mathematics, he joined Alcan UK as a Graduate Trainee and was eventually transferred to the Rogerstone plant, just outside Newport, where he rose to Logistics Manager. He and his wife, Rosemary, had three sons, each of whom attended St. Joseph's.

Phase I Activity

The first battle after convincing the authorities, both State and Church, that there was a need for such a school was to establish a site for it. Suggestions were made by the LEA for a start to the project at St. Andrew's School, a Victorian building on Corporation Road. It was maintained that there were no funds available in the Capital Building Programme. The Church authorities were also concerned at the cost, having to contribute 15% to the building costs. The Association objected to this suggestion knowing that *"parity of esteem"* with modern purpose-built schools was imperative to attract children of the highest abilities to a newly established school.

In October 1966, the Association wrote to Archbishop John Murphy asking for his assistance to establish the School, and to receive a deputation. In reply, His Grace outlined problems of access being put up by the Ministry of Transport to Tredegar House, the favoured site for the new school. Also the cost of temporary classrooms to get the school started was such that he could not justify meeting it from diocesan funds.

He agreed rather reluctantly to meet a deputation in St. Mary's Presbytery, Stow Hill, Newport, during his parochial visit in May 1967. There were six committee members present representing the Association, all standing when His Grace entered the room. Without ado, he strongly pointed out the cost of our aims to the diocese, and walked along the line-up of members wagging his finger to all. Quite a forceful presence!

However, the parents' wishes prevailed, and the site was established in the grounds of Tredegar House. This was assisted by a far-sighted move by the Nuns, who not only made the land available, but also financed the two terrapin buildings, which enabled Phase I of the School to start with the requisite number of classrooms in September 1967. Tredegar House, which until that time had housed St. Joseph's Convent High School, was the initial base for the School.

Conscious that St. Joseph's would be a comprehensive school in line with Government policy, the Association arranged talks for parents by firstly Mr. Raymond Jones, Headmaster of Hartridge

High School, Newport, and next by Mr. J. Rudden, Headmaster of Bishop Thomas Grant R.C. School, London. These talks were attended by large numbers of interested parents who took the opportunity to question the speakers about this new form of education.

The Association recognised that it was essential that Catholic parents in Newport and South Gwent gave their full support to the new school by sending their children there.

Phase II Activity

It was in December 1968 that the news broke that Phase II was to be postponed until 1974 or later. The Chief Education Officer (CEO) for Newport stated that *"In 1970/71 the LEA hope to see some essential projects start but this does not include any R.C. Schools"*. He later stated *"the LEA is not able to support an early start on the building of Phase II . . . in their view there is a greater need for an early start on other local projects"*.

A deputation consisting of representatives of the Association and the Governors had a meeting with the CEO and Chairman of the Education Committee to appeal against this decision, but the appeal was rejected by the Schools' Development Committee of the LEA.

Subsequently, the Association decided to organise a public meeting of parents to explain the situation and enrol their support. The meeting was held in the King's Head Hotel, Newport, on 20th October 1969, and was attended by some 400 people. It was resolved at the meeting to:

- Write to Archbishop Murphy for his support;
- Approach Mr. Roy Hughes, M.P. for Newport and Mr. Donald Anderson, M.P. for Monmouth;

- Organise a petition to present to the then Minister of Education, Mr. Edward Short, M.P.

Petition forms were printed and distributed to each parish for signing at Mass. Subsequently the petition, containing some 3,300 signatures, was sent to Mr. Short, the Minister. In addition, a formal objection under the 1944 Education Act was made to the Newport LEA's notice of intention to build a comprehensive School at Nash, giving it priority over Phase II of St. Joseph's.

Emotions at the time were running high; the following report appeared in the *South Wales Argus*:

R.C. High School delay sparks Newport row

Pupils in Roman Catholic primary schools in Newport are being treated as "children of second class citizens" when it comes to allocating places in high schools, claim Catholic parents' association.

Newport Corporation are treating the children unfairly and not making enough places available for higher education, it was claimed at a meeting called by the Catholic Parents' and Electors' Association. The building programme on the only Catholic-run high school in the town – St. Joseph's – has been half completed and now delayed for two years, it was stated.

They say this action had led to a definite deficiency of places for children leaving Catholic primary Schools

To ask M.P.

The meeting, attended by nearly 400 people, set up an action committee and decided to ask Mr. Roy Hughes, M.P., to intervene on their behalf.

When Newport Council agreed to extend St. Joseph's School it was planned to finish before the fifth comprehensive school was ready. This was accepted by the Ministry of Education. The work on phase one, providing less than 600 places, under half the total need, was begun.

Last year phase two was put back two years in the building programme and the comprehensive School, which had had a lesser priority, was to be built sooner.

Deficiency

Mr. Alan Shewring, a governor of St. Joseph's, said the situation had developed into crisis proportions and without a Catholic school some children would be seriously affected.

The Headmaster, Mr. J. Witherington, said that with the number of pupils leaving primary schools during the next four years, those requiring Catholic education would find a definite deficiency of places.

The Chairman, Mr. Aubrey Hames, said it appeared that the local authority was bent on treating Catholic pupils as "children of second class citizens".

A six-point resolution to put to the Council was agreed and this was supported by 350 signatures.

In the period from January 1970, there was a great deal of correspondence between the Association and the politicians mentioned above, that culminated in a meeting with the Right Honourable Peter Thomas, M.P., Secretary of State for Wales. A joint deputation from the Association and the Governors of St. Joseph's met with the Minister and his advisers at the Mansion House in Newport. (This meeting is referred to in the section on "*Construction Phases*").

In December 1970, the growing crisis was reported in the *South Wales Echo*:

Lack of room may force Newport R.C. School to close

Roman Catholic education authorities have warned the Welsh Office that they will be forced to close down St. Joseph's High School, Newport, unless further accommodation is provided by September 1973.

"By that date the number of pupils in the School will have exceeded the 900 places and we will have to cease to function unless the second phase of the complex is built", said Mr. Alan Shewring, a governor of the School, today.

The Right Rev. Daniel Mullins, Auxiliary Bishop of Cardiff and Chairman of the Diocesan Education Commission, has written to the Secretary of State for Wales warning that the School will have to be closed unless the second stage is proceeded with without delay.

A deputation from the governors and Catholic Parents' and Electors' Association will meet the Secretary of State, Mr. Peter Thomas, on 8th January, to plead for the £600,000 second stage of the School to be included in the building programme.

St. Joseph's was reorganised as a comprehensive complex in 1967. Work on the building of the first phase started at Tredegar Park in November 1968, and the project cost £267,000. The first and the second forms for boys and girls are housed in two old schools in Newport, some three miles from the main School, which now has 600 pupils enrolled.

By using Tredegar House, a former private school, St. Joseph's can accommodate 900 pupils at Tredegar Park but by the autumn of 1973 the estimated School population will be 940, and in the following year will exceed 1,000.

In reply to the Association's petition, a letter was received from the Department of Education and Science at the Welsh Office explaining that due to a Governmental Review, school building programmes had been revised. Priority was to be given to projects designed to provide places where none existed over the replacement of existing schools. As a result, Phase II of St. Joseph's which was to replace the existing Junior High Schools, was to be deferred until April 1972. However, it added, since that decision had been taken, the Government had announced that limited resources could now be made available for a limited number of projects for the improvement or replacement of existing schools. Further, that the Governors had asked the LEA to include the St. Joseph's project in their submission for this allocation, which was in respect of the building programme 1971/72.

The Governors were informed that their submission had been placed top of the priority list of submissions for Wales, and that building of Phase II could commence in 1971.

Regarding the objections to Nash School, it had been pointed out by the Welsh Office that in view of the LEA's recent decision to make changes in the organisation of the Newport School involving the provision of a sixth form college, such proposals would radically affect the composition of Nash School and therefore the LEA had been advised that the notices for Nash School must be regarded as withdrawn and a fresh notice should be published forthwith.

There was a deep sense of relief in the Association at this news, and it was felt that finally the long struggle to get the School built was succeeding.

SISTERS OF ST. JOSEPH
OF ANNECY

The founding of the Congregation

The Sisters of St. Joseph were founded in 1650, at Le Puy, France. A Jesuit priest, Father Medaille, grouped together a small band of women who wished to dedicate their lives to God in the service of the poor. They themselves had no money to enable them to enter an established Order where a dowry was necessary. Father Medaille's *"Little Design"*, as he called it, offered them the means of fulfilling their deep desires. He wrote rules for them, proposed St. Joseph as their patron and called them *"Daughters of St. Joseph"*. Father Medaille broke through barriers by establishing a Congregation in which the members would be contemplatives in action, going out to help all those most in need.

The Congregation grew rapidly but had a chequered history during the French Revolution and the years immediately following. However, after the dispersal of the Sisters during the years of the Revolution, they were re-grouped and established once again in various parts of France, taking the name of the diocese in which their main house was established. With the foundations in Annecy, the Sisters became officially known as Sisters of St. Joseph of Annecy in 1833.

The English Mission

The Congregation spread, and their first mission in India was established in 1849. From there, due to the initiative and generosity of an officer in the British Army, the Sisters came to England in 1864 and settled in Devizes, Wiltshire, supporting the work of the two priests there, Missionaries of St. Francis de Sales, with whom the Sisters had worked in India. The first three Sisters comprised: Sister Athanase Novel (French), Sister Stanislaus Bryan (whose father was an Irish soldier in India), and Sister Josephine Twomey who had been teaching in Chippenham before entering with the Sisters at Annecy. Beginnings were hard. Local hostility which extended even to stoning the Sisters as they went about their work of serving the poor, offering education to the children, and generally trying to meet the needs of the most neglected, did not deter their determination to persevere in this new mission.

A large house had been purchased to accommodate two priests who were setting up a Mass Centre in a disused warehouse in the town. But the priests moved out to allow the Sisters to live there and open a small school. Despite these extremely hard beginnings the English mission flourished and expanded. The expansion came about by developments in education in England and Wales. Due to the provisions of the Education Act 1870, it was deemed necessary by Catholic Authorities to establish Catholic schools in which religion could be taught. State Schools, previously known as Board Schools, which were maintained through the rates, were not allowed to teach religion. Denominational schools could receive limited assistance from central government and retain the right to teach religion. These schools were called Voluntary Aided Schools.

In 1873 the Sisters were invited to Newport by Father Michael Bailey, a Rosminian priest, who had heard of the Sisters from his own sister, a Visitation nun in Westbury. This led to the establishment of the English Province in 1882.

Involvement in education in Newport

At the time that the 1870 Act came into force there were two schools at St. Mary's, Newport: a boys' school where a Rosminian brother,

Brother George Clarkson taught and was Headmaster, and a girls' school where three Sisters of Providence taught. It was decided, that in order to comply with the Act, the two schools would have to amalgamate. However, Brother George was getting on in years, and the Sisters of Providence were debarred, by their Rule, from teaching boys.

In 1871 there were over a thousand Catholic children in Newport and so a school was built in St. Michael's Parish to alleviate the problem of over-crowding. The School Managers, who were the parish priests, paid the teachers salaries which were *"what the priest could afford"*. Moreover, the Managers had to provide furniture and books. Although parental contributions were requested, they were not always forthcoming. The problem was serious, and teachers did not want to come to Newport because of the difficult conditions.

Father Bailey, who at that time was a curate at St. Mary's, heard through his sister of the good work the Devizes Sisters were doing at Westbury. He visited the Sisters at Devizes and suggested that Newport was the opportunity the Sisters were looking for. He was delighted when Mother Athanase wrote to say she was really interested. He immediately approached his parish priest, Father Cavalli, to agree to the Sisters coming to Newport. A house, at 89 Stow Hill came on to the market in 1873, and Mother Athanase purchased it for £1,600. This property eventually became the Provincial House and also housed the Convent School. But since this house would not become vacant for eighteen months, the Sisters lodged initially with a Mrs. Cappella in Commercial Street, at the place where Marks and Spencer now stands.

The Sisters of Providence had held their classes in the Institute, the building next to St. Mary's, Stow Hill, before withdrawing from the school in 1873. Meanwhile, the Sisters of St. Joseph had moved to Newport, leaving only two Sisters and a postulant in Devizes. The school in the Institute occupied the ground floor, with some of the Sisters being lodged on the upper floor. So began the long associa-

13

tion of the Sisters of St. Joseph with St. Mary's, to the benefit of generations of children. Eventually, the Sisters were able to occupy 89 Stow Hill and the convent vacated by the Sisters of Providence became St. Mary's Presbytery, which it is to this day. In 1875, the Sisters of St. Joseph withdrew from Westbury to make Newport the centre of the English Province.

By the end of the Second World War, accommodation at Stow Hill had expanded with the acquisition of new buildings. Nevertheless, it had become too crowded, housing a large community of Sisters and a boarding and day school for girls. It was necessary, therefore, to look for other premises. In 1946, Llantarnam Abbey came on the market, and despite its dilapidated state, the Sisters bought it and set about renovating it. It became, and is, the Provincial House, providing accommodation for a fairly large community, which, at that time, included about twelve Sisters who were teaching in the primary schools in Newport.

The next step came when, in spite of the move to Llantarnam Abbey, space in the school on Stow Hill became a problem yet again and it seemed that the secondary sector of the school should be separated from the primary sector. Search for other premises started and when Tredegar House came on the market, the Sisters bought it in 1951. For one year, before the actual transfer of the school, a few Sisters lived there and gradually prepared the house for its future use. The Senior School took up residence there in September 1952, and developed into a flourishing boarding and day school. It remained as such until the Comprehensive School was established in 1967.

St. Joseph's Convent High School for Girls

The private school at Tredegar Park admitted a considerable number of Catholic girls who had passed the 11+ examination, without charging them fees. With changes in education policies and the move towards

17th Century frontage of Tredegar House with Edney gates.

*Magazine cover for the Convent School
located at Tredegar House.*

15

comprehensive education, Newport LEA agreed to pay the fees, each year, for 20 girls, until such time as there would be enough places in their own newly organised local comprehensive schools. This move, coupled with the continuing policy of the Sisters to offer a number of free places, ensured current Catholic secondary education. It was becoming more and more evident that this could not continue, even from the financial point of view of the Sisters who were finding it increasingly difficult to maintain this policy. Although the move by the LEA was primarily for their own benefit, it was a welcome bonus for the school at Tredegar Park. It was obvious that the future of the school lay either in opting for the comprehensive system or changing its ethos.

Negotiations had been going on, in the background, for some time, to opt for comprehensive education for all Catholic children in Newport. But, for the Sisters, the first positive move came when they offered land at Tredegar Park for the proposed new school. Once this had been accepted, and decision made, there were a number of consequences to be faced in the period 1966/67:

- Notice to be given to parents of boarders who came from different parts of Great Britain and even a few from France, Spain and Switzerland;

- Provision for non-Catholic pupils living in the County and for whom – except those in their last year before O and A Level Examinations – Newport Authorities refused to provide in the new comprehensive school;

- Visits by Sister Pauline and Sister Mary Patrick, Head and Deputy Head of the Convent School, to already established comprehensive schools in other parts of the country (Coventry, Bristol, London and South Wales) to learn from others' experience.

The visits to comprehensive schools already operating, allowed Sister Pauline and Sister Mary Patrick to explore the various ways of organising the school. They examined the merits and demerits of organising horizontally on a Year system or vertically on a House system. When it was decided that Sister Mary Patrick would take a temporary teaching post at Bishop Thomas Grant School in London, where the Year system operated, it gave the opportunity for studying this method in more detail. Sister Pauline also spent some time at this school and finally the Year system was adopted as the more acceptable of the two. In this, a Head of Year would have a determined area of authority and be able to organise his year group as a mini Head, in consultation with the administrative staff of the whole school.

Having agreed on a site for building the new School, the lack of immediate and adequate accommodation for the optimum opening date of September 1967, created grave problems. The proposals to continue using the two Secondary Modern Schools as Junior High Schools until such times as the building at Tredegar Park was completed, and Tredegar House for the 13-18 year ranges, were dragged out. Eventually Sister Pauline went to London with Mother Finbarr (the Provincial Superior) and Canon Luke Delaney (representing the Cardiff Archdiocese) to a pre-arranged meeting at Curzon Street, with Mrs. Shirley Williams, the Minister of Education.

Some tough talking ensued but no decision was made. It had been stressed that a start had to be made by September 1967. A telephone call, received on the 6th May 1967, gave Sister Pauline the news that the *"go-ahead"* had been granted to start the new school in September of that year, thus giving four months to wind down, not one, but three schools, and prepare for another, on three different sites, and of a completely different educational style. Consequently the Convent School at Tredegar Park closed earlier than scheduled in July, and after that it was a case of all hands on deck! Dormitories, occupied by boarders, needed to be cleared, and furniture to be disposed of. The erection of two pre-fabricated buildings to provide four extra classrooms, and a small army of workmen for the various odd jobs for the relocation and renovation within Tredegar House ensued. Somehow, by foregoing any sort of Summer holiday and with determination and a daily supply of willing workers from among the Sisters at Llantarnam Abbey, Tredegar House was made ready and the school did open on time in September 1967. The birth of the new school entailed the Convent School handing over lock, stock and barrel, in terms of equipment and furniture. The first school assembly, of 500+ pupils, boys and girls – (13-18 age groups) – took place in the old Riding School, the only building large enough to house the expanded number. It would be several years before a School Hall would be built.

Sister Pauline

Sister Pauline was born in Risca, Monmouthshire, and educated at St. Joseph's Convent School, Stow Hill, Newport. She entered the novitiate of the Sisters of St. Joseph after school but not before she had spent 18 months at home, by that time at Weymouth, doing mostly voluntary wartime work. When she had completed her novitiate period she spent two years at Southampton Training College for Teachers, at the time, evacuated to Cheltenham because of wartime conditions. Having obtained her teacher's certificate she went immediately from college to Manchester University to read for a science degree in Geography and Mathematics.

On completion of her degree course she returned to her old school at Stow Hill and began her teaching career of 32 years. This was in the same school that she had attended as a pupil, located firstly at Stow Hill, and then at Tredegar House, and finally on the new site of the Comprehensive School. The name of St. Joseph's High School was common to each School, and provided the link in 100 years of tradition since the Sisters first came to Newport.

*Sister Pauline receiving Communion from Bishop Mullins
on the occasion of her retirement.*

Presentation by Chairman of Governors, Alan Shewring.

Cutting the Cake.

Bishop Mullins, the Chairman, Member of Staff Edward Curran, and Guests.

Eventually she succeeded Sister St. Brendan as Headmistress of the Convent High School and remained in post until the Convent School closed in the Summer of 1967.

The shortage of time remaining, once the go-ahead was given, left little opportunity for advertising and appointing a Head of the new Comprehensive School. The Senior School was to be started in Tredegar House and the Heads of the former Secondary Modern Schools were to remain as Heads of the new Junior High Schools. It was logical therefore that Sister Pauline would be Acting-Head of the Senior Section until such time that a Head could be formally appointed. She held this position for the first two terms of the newly created School and was happy to hand over the Headship to Mr. Joseph Witherington, who had been appointed to take up his responsibility in May 1968. She had no wish to be ultimately responsible for a school with an envisaged roll of 1,600 pupils. She held the post of First Deputy Head until her early retirement in December 1980, when she undertook responsibility for the formation of young Sisters in the Province.

Having laid the foundations with the initial planning and setting up of the academic and pastoral structures of St. Joseph's High School, Sister Pauline and Sister Mary Patrick left a legacy which is still serving succeeding generations of pupils and staff.

THE SCHOOL OPENS

Administrative arrangements

St. Joseph's High School commenced in September 1967, operating from three sites. The Senior School for pupils aged 13-18 was based at Tredegar House, recently vacated by St. Joseph's Convent High School; the Junior High School for Boys aged 11-13 was based at the former Father Hill Secondary School in Oswald Road; and the Junior High School for Girls aged 11-13 was based at the former Holy Family Secondary School at Emlyn Street.

Each of the Schools had its own Headteacher; Sister Pauline was Acting-Head of the Senior School, Bernard Dunn continued as Head of the Junior Boys' School and Sister Madeleine Sophie was Head of the Junior Girls' School.

Voluntary aided status

Under the dual system established by the Education Acts 1944 et seq., church schools are afforded special rights and duties whilst being maintained by LEAs. Staff salaries are paid by the LEAs as well as maintenance, furniture, equipment and books. The churches are responsible for the building of the school and external maintenance, although this expenditure attracts government grants of 85% of the total costs.

These rights were hard-won and it was imperative that they were exercised responsibly and with care. The fact that eight of the twelve governors were foundation governors, i.e. appointed by the Church, was to ensure that the character and ethos of the School was preserved and developed, and to ensure that the School was conducted in accordance with the provisions of the Trust Deed.

It is not generally appreciated that in voluntary aided church schools the governors are the employers of the staff and have responsibility for the conduct and curriculum of the school. These onerous duties are carried out, of course, in full consultation with the head teacher, who controls the day-to-day internal organisation, management and discipline of the school. The position of aided secondary schools is different from that of county and controlled schools in that in aided schools, secular and religious instruction is under the control of the governors.

The interviewing and appointment of teachers is one of the most challenging and difficult duties governors have to perform. As employers of the staff, it is essential that a representative number of governors are involved in appointments.

The Board of Governors

The governors were installed, eight foundation governors appointed by Archbishop John Murphy and four borough councillors nominated by Newport LEA, although initially only three took up their appointments. Alan Shewring's appointment as a Foundation Governor was in recognition of the CPEA, a nice gesture by His Grace.

Foundation Governors

Monsignor Daniel Mullins
Reverend Mother Finbarr
Reverend Wilfred Davies, I.C.
Reverend Luke Delaney

Reverend Tom Donovan
J. Alan Shewring
Thomas G. Price
Dr. Catherine Hayes

LEA Representative Governors

> Alderman Mrs. Mary Dunn
> Councillor A. G. Lovell
> Alderman Sidney Millar

The formal elections of Chairman and Vice-Chairman and appointment of Clerk to the Governors did not actually take place until the first proper meeting of Governors on 22nd May 1968. Alderman Mrs. Mary Dunn was elected Chairman due to the prompt actions of the LEA Governors. This was unusual, as it was normal for a Foundation Governor to be Chairman; however, Mary Dunn was accepted, as she was a prominent Catholic.

Father Wilfred Davies, a Rosminian priest, was elected Vice-Chairman. Father Davies was well respected in education circles as a former headmaster. Unfortunately, he met with a fatal car accident on New Year's Eve 1969.

Mary Dunn was Chairman until ill-health forced her retirement in 1973, at which time Alan Shewring was elected Chairman.

Monsignor Mullins was Clerk to the Governors in the early years. He was subsequently elevated to Auxiliary Bishop of Cardiff. Governors' meetings were held in the splendour of the Gilt Room in Tredegar House, although a mis-typing invited the builder, Noel T. James, to meet the Governors in the *"Guilt"* Room to explain the delays in the building programme!

After Bishop Mullins resigned from the Governors in 1974, the role of Clerk was, by force of circumstances, taken up by the Chairman, who fulfilled this responsibility until his retirement in 1991, apart from a few years when Father Peter Eedy did the clerking. In the early years the business of getting the School built occupied the prime place on the agenda, but there were always a multitude of matters to attend to, including the appointment of staff as the School grew in size. The School's roll reached its highest point in 1979 with approximately 1,650 pupils. In that year alone the Chairman spent some 15 working days in School on interviews and meetings. This was fairly typical for life as Chairman of Governors, and it meant working evenings and week-ends to keep abreast of commitments in the busy and expanding accountancy practice in which he was a partner.

The problems and struggles seemed endless:

- Negotiations for playing fields;
- Transport arrangements;
- Car parking;
- Drainage problems;
- Negotiations for the exchange of land with Newport Borough Council;
- Access and egress to the School;
- Meetings, meetings and more meetings.

The correspondence in all of this was considerable, and it was fortunate that the Chairman had the secretarial resources in his office to enable this to be done.

The first meeting of the Governors was to interview applicants for the Headship. The interviews were held in the Civic Centre, Newport, in December 1967, and the Governors were assisted and advised by the Chief Education Officer, Mr. E. H. Loudon. Sixteen applicants were interviewed, coming from various parts of the U.K., and Mr. Joseph Witherington was appointed. He was at that time Head of a School in Hull, Yorkshire, and took up his post as Head of St.

Joseph's in May 1968, after giving the requisite notice. Sister Pauline, the Acting-Head, did not apply for the post.

Pupils on roll

In his first Headmaster's Report at the Meeting of Governors on 22nd May 1968 Mr. Witherington included details of the School roll for September 1968:

1st Year	2nd Year	3rd Year	4th Year	5th Year	6th Year	Total
237	214	153	152	65	60	**881**

His Report also gave projections for the next six years:

1969	1970	1971	1972	1973	1974
1,035	1,204	1,440	1,540	1,620	1,700

Although these were estimations based on an annual intake of 300 pupils from 1970 onwards, they did underline the crisis in accommodation that would occur unless the School buildings were completed as planned. The School's roll ultimately reached its maximum in 1979. It was a very large school by any criteria! In fact, at that point St. Joseph's was the second largest Catholic comprehensive school in the U.K.

Staffing

In the same Report, the Head gave the following details of staffing:

	Senior School	Junior Boys' School	Junior Girls' School	Total
Male	10	8	1	19
Female	21	2	13	36
	31	**10**	**14**	**55**

The following staff appointments were made on 22nd May 1968, the interviews taking place during the Governors' Meeting:

Senior School: Messrs. Frank Batty; Peter Morgan; S. Thomas

Junior Boys' School: Messrs. Davies; Michael Farley; Dermot Flude; Miss Langford

Junior Girls School: Mr. Rees; Miss Pritchard; Sister Ursula; Barbara Langley

Part Time: Mrs. Basset; Mrs. Cohen.

Staff List 1968/69

Headmaster: J. Witherington, B.A., Dip.Ed.

Deputy Head: Sister. M. Pauline, B.Sc., Dip.Ed.

Second Master: F. M. Batty, B.A., Dip.Ed.

Director of Studies: Sister Mary Patrick, Ph.D., B.A., Dip.Ed.

The appointments made in the early years and a full staffing list is included in Appendix 2.

When the three Schools were brought together onto the one site the year system for pastoral care and discipline was fully operational. Gerry Drewett, Ted Richards, Brian McCann and Eileen Connolley did sterling work as Heads of Year, most of them for over 20 years. They dealt with all problems and were the contact point for parents, and were generally responsible for the day-to-day care of the pupils. The size of their responsibility can be measured by the numbers in their year groups that averaged 300 pupils. Pastoral care had by this time become a major undertaking in all secondary schools. The School was most fortunate to have had staff of this calibre who gave so much of themselves in the daily life of St. Joseph's. Each Head of Year had an Assistant Head. Paddy Landers, who was one of those Assistant Heads of Year, has since risen to Deputy Headteacher of the School. Frank Batty, who died tragically young, made a significant contribution in his brief time at the School as Second Master. It should be mentioned that Gerry Drewett was Deputy Head of the Junior Boys' High School until the merger in 1974, and was Acting-Head for a period whilst the Head, Bernard Dunn, retrained for primary education.

The School had some outstanding subject teachers, whose efforts and talents revealed themselves in increasingly good examination results. Maggie Kreuser set very high standards as Head of English and was a remarkably inspiring teacher as were other department heads: Peter Waters (Physics); Lyn Evans (Biology); Pat Thomas (French); Peter Stevenson (Design, Craft and Technology); Mostyn Bennett (Sixth Form and Director of Studies); Eric Bryant (Group Studies); and Pat Jenkins (Mathematics).

We were fortunate to have found such an able successor to Sister Pauline as First Deputy Head in Dr. David Neville. As well as being a Graduate in Chemistry, David had a Doctorate in Music and is Master of the Music and organist at the Metropolitan Cathedral of St. David's in Cardiff. He subsequently left the School to set up St. John's College in Cardiff, a highly successful independent school catering for pupils from four to 18 years of age.

The Senior High School (Tredegar House)

Headteacher: Joseph Witherington, B.A., Dip.Ed.

Deputy Headteacher: Sister M. Pauline, B.Sc., Dip.Ed.

Joseph Witherington took up the Headship in May 1968, based in Tredegar House with the construction of Phase I of the new school about to commence on the area of land provided by the Sisters of St. Joseph. He made his first Report to Governors at their meeting in November 1968; the following are excerpts from the Head's Report in those early years:

7th November 1968

Curriculum. *The streaming prevalent in the Junior High Schools is at present maintained in the Senior School. Setting to be started in Autumn 1968 in two broad bands. An integrated curriculum is being tried out with the two lower streams in 3rd and 4th years. Project work and social education are the bases of this curriculum. Reactions of staff and pupils are favourable. "A" Level courses are at present offered in English; French; History; Mathematics; Latin; Physics; Chemistry; Botany; Zoology; Art; Geography; Economics; British Constitution; Sociology. "O" Level Italian to be offered in the VI Form.*

23rd June 1969

Buildings. *Phase I well underway with the House Block due to be ready for September with the completion of the Assembly Hall and Gymnasium by late November. The Practical Block is expected to be ready by Easter 1970. Plans for converting two Terrapin units into Physics and Chemistry laboratories are under consideration.*

28th June 1970

1969/70 was, I hope, the most trying and difficult in the history of the School. The inconvenience caused by the long distances to be covered between lessons from Tredegar House to the new buildings under erection across what was often a morass of mud has been borne willingly, even cheerfully, by all the staff.

3rd November 1970

Strain on accommodation and all rooms in Tredegar House have to be used as form bases and teaching spaces. The situation will be eased after Christmas on completion of the Practical Block.

1st July 1971

Buildings. *Terrapins have been in use since Easter. Excellent as laboratories and very well equipped. The stables will not be used at all in September (for safety reasons). The top floor of Tredegar House will not be used for general school purposes.*

19th June 1973

Head explained impossibility of running the School with a roll of 900 plus in the existing premises, reduced as they are by the loss of eight rooms in Tredegar House.

15th October 1973

Start of academic year presented the worst problems of accommodation yet. Enormous amount of time wasted in the long trek round muddy paths between old and new buildings.

13th May 1974

Sister Madeleine Sophie has tendered her resignation as Head of Junior High School for Girls.

Bernard Dunn was recently appointed to Headship of St. Joseph's Primary School, and had tendered his resignation as Head of the Junior High School for Boys.

Monica Thomas, Deputy Head of the Junior Girls' High School, was retiring.

3rd October 1974

Buildings. *Term started in very bad weather with twelve teaching spaces short due to the failure of the Terrapin firm to complete the work they began in June, and that of the builders to finish the Laboratories in the Science Block.*

Examination Results. *As is shown by the detailed analysis results were by far the best we have had.*

The report given by the Head shewed that eight pupils went to University, including two to Oxford – Ruth Pitchford and Goretti Lai; four pupils went to Teacher Training Colleges; three pupils to Polytechnics; and eleven pupils to Colleges of Further Education.

24th May 1976

The Sixth Form Suite *(Phase III) a very handsome building, was handed over on Friday, 14th May, and occupied 17th May 1976.*

Playing Field Site. *Work will commence . . . . ?*

13th October 1976

For the first time ever the School opened in September with a full complement of teaching staff and with all buildings complete and all parts of them ready for use.

There has been an atmosphere of ease, security – even serenity – about the beginning of this academic year; a difference noted by a number of staff.

Examination Results
'A' Level produced the highest ever number of passes and a remarkable increase in the number of 'A', 'B' and 'C' grades.

55 boys and girls attained five or more "O" Level passes each.

Head Girl, Ursula O'Reilly, has been interviewed for a place at Hertford College, Oxford. The Head Boy, Philip Constable, is applying to Downing College, Cambridge. (N.B. Both were successful, and subsequently took up their places)

JOSEPH WITHERINGTON

No account of St. Joseph's High School would be complete without due tribute being paid to this taciturn, kindly and scholarly Yorkshireman. Mr. Witherington was not a gregarious man but he dedicated himself, almost to the exclusion of all else, to the management and development of St. Joseph's. His philosophy was traditional and the School was organised academically by streaming and setting. This produced outstanding examination successes by the mid to late 1970s. In the 1980s the strict streaming gave way to banding.

He contracted a fatal illness and died on 21st March 1988, whilst still Headmaster. He was very respected in educational circles, and will always be associated with the development of the School.

The Junior High School for Girls (Emlyn Street)

Headteacher: Sister Madeleine Sophie, B.A.

Deputy Headteacher: Monica Thomas, T.Cert.

Sister Madeleine Sophie was Headteacher from September 1967 until her retirement in July 1974. A gentle, sensitive person, she suffered great anxieties for the well being of staff and pupils during her time as Head in the sub-standard premises in Emlyn Street. Her concerns were expressed from time to time in her Reports to Governors, extracts from which follow:

3rd October 1969

Organisation. *Pupils are arranged in ten forms, with the first two groups parallel in ability, the third and fourth groups likewise and the fifth group in each year a remedial class.*

3rd November 1970

Buildings. *School suffering not only with problems of space but also break-ins, and, with redevelopment in the surrounding area, heavy traffic and noise.*

25th March 1971

Accommodation lacking in September 1971. *Form space – one: Home economics: Toilets.*

Inadequacies. *External toilets with no wash basins: Playground Spaces: Canteen: Staff accommodation.*

Environment. *Heavy traffic. Noise. Health and Safety. Derelict buildings adjacent utilised by vagrants.*

Toilets. *Only seven toilets, all external; no heating; no hand-basins. In severe weather pipes freeze.*

Classrooms. *In 1971 there will be four "floating classes" because no classrooms are available for class bases.*

Ceilings and walls damaged by damp. Room sizes inadequate.

Mary Williams, formerly on the staff of the Junior Girls' High School, recalls those early years with nostalgia.

Sister Madeleine Sophie managed the small staff in a kindly but firm manner, and the School was a warm and encouraging place for staff and pupils. Staff were occasionally allowed an extended lunch in town, when Sisters Madeleine and Ursula took the whole School for hymn singing in the Hall.

An annual event was the "*Glee Club*" in which girls could perform either individually or in groups, and each production had a theme. The rehearsals were supervised by Mrs. Lynn Brown assisted by other staff members. In those early days, prior to the pressures of the National Curriculum, rehearsals took place during School time. These were events eagerly anticipated by staff and pupils and were a source of great enjoyment to all.

The late 1960s and early 1970s saw the rise in popularity of the Folk Mass, and these Masses were a feature of School life, with the girls taking part on guitars, violins and flutes.

Being a comparatively small school, comprising only two years, there was an intimate atmosphere with all pupils known by the staff, rather like a large family.

Mary transferred to the Tredegar House site together with other staff when the three Schools merged in 1974, and eventually retired in 2003.

The Junior High School for Boys
(Oswald Road, Pillgwenlly)

Headteacher: Bernard Dunn, T.Cert.

Deputy Headteacher: Gerry Drewett, B.A.

Bernard Dunn was a well-respected and popular Head and good disciplinarian with a strong concern for his staff. As had his counterpart in the Girls' Junior High, he made known his concerns in reports to the Governors.

30th October 1969

Accommodation. *Use of the Gymnasium at Belle Vue School commenced in September 1969.*

Organisation. *First year pupils are now grouped in two bands, each band consisting of two forms of equal ability, within each band setting in Mathematics, French and English is organised.*

23rd February 1970

Conditions over the last three months proved to be unusually trying for pupils. The very wet weather has made lunchtime journeys to Belle Vue School Canteen miserable excursions. Mr. Farley, our P.E. Master, has paddled his way uncomplainingly to the Belle Vue Gymnasium, making more than eight journeys on some days. Teachers are commended for their loyalty and sterling qualities.

Accommodation. *The anticipated roll for September 1970 is 260 boys – ten form bases. Only nine form bases are available. I recommend that the Art Room is used as a form base and Art is done at YMCA if CEO is agreeable.*

25th June 1970

Deep apprehension concerning future use of accommodation at Belle Vue School. It seems certain that in early 1971 the LEA will re-house Alexandra Road Infants and Junior Schools at Belle Vue. This could mean the loss of use of an Art Room and Gymnasium, facilities essential to the life of the School.

3rd November 1970

Due to the increased roll the Hall must now serve for multipurposes including Drama Workshop, Music Room, Band Practice, etc., etc., as well as Assembly.

25th March 1971

Deficiencies – 1971 onwards. 1 Gymnasium; 1 Form Base; 1 Art Room.

Inadequacies. Cloakroom and drying facilities; External toilets; Canteen facilities; Library; Film Room; Music Room; Play Space; Storage Space.

Mike Farley and Alan Kethro recall with affection those early years at the Junior Boys' High School, when they were both newly qualified teachers.

Before playtime, Bernard Dunn used to ask staff to sweep the hard play area free of broken glass from the local youths. On hot summer days, in times when timetables were not so pressurised as today, the Head would extend break times and send a boy across to a lady living nearby who made ice-cream. A large box full of ice creams would then appear for the staff to enjoy: "*I thought this would be a good idea*", the Head would say.

The end of term staff party was an event enjoyed by all when Kitty Dunn, the Head's wife, always provided tea, sandwiches and cakes. Again, St. Joseph's Day was celebrated by the whole School with Mass at nearby St. Michael's Church, after which chocolate bars were issued to each boy. This had to be collected from the Head by proffering the school cap to receive it. Caps, which were in short supply, were passed behind backs along the line up of boys!

Mike and Alan agreed these were very happy times, and they could not have wished for a better or more enjoyable start to their careers.

The move to the new School in 1974 saw a marked contrast in facilities from the Junior Boys' School with its open corridors and very basic amenities, to the superb Gymnasium, Art Rooms, Science

Presentation to Sister Carmel on her Retirement by the Chairman of Governors,
Alan Shewring, on 31st October 1978. In background,Mr. Joseph Witherington,
Sister Pauline and Members of the Governing Body.

Laboratories, and much else of the new School. The setting of the
new School also was idyllic being adjacent to the lake and grounds
of Tredegar House.

They remarked that the presence of the Nuns at the School was
greatly missed, and Mike recalled his surprise at Sister Carmel super-
vising football out on the playing fields wearing hockey boots under
her habit!

Both Alan and Mike are still teaching at St. Joseph's having given
over 35 years service to the School.

When, finally, the three schools were amalgamated on to one site
in September 1974, and the two Junior High Schools vacated, there
was the thorny problem of merging the staffs of the three schools
and the complexities and sensitivities of posts and salaries to be

resolved. The Chairman of Governors found himself in the position of mediator and negotiator in this difficult situation and a meeting was held at Bishop Mullins' residence in Penarth between His Lordship, the Chairman and the Heads of the Junior High Schools, Sister Madeleine Sophie and Bernard Dunn. Joseph Witherington was unable to attend due to illness. Consequently it was necessary for the Chairman and Bishop Mullins to familiarise themselves with the scale points system and an agreement was brokered with the Heads to resolve the issue.

CONSTRUCTION PHASES

Phase I

The School was built in three phases. Phase I comprising the House Block, Assembly Hall, Gymnasium and Practical Block was physically started in November 1969, and completed in the spring of 1970. The School was officially opened on 5th May 1970 by Mr. Edward Short, M.P., the then Secretary of State for Education in a ceremony presided over by Archbishop John Murphy. The ceremony was held in the newly built Assembly Hall.

The Governors of St. Joseph's High School
request the pleasure of the company of

Mr. & Mrs. J. A. Shewring

at the

OFFICIAL OPENING of PHASE I

by THE RT. HON. EDWARD SHORT, M. P.
Secretary of State for Education and Science

and the

DEDICATION

by THE MOST REV. JOHN A. MURPHY, D.D.
Archbishop of Cardiff

2. 30 p.m.   TUESDAY, 5th MAY, 1970

R S V.P.
The Right Rev. D. J. Mullins B. A.
Auxiliary Bishop in the Archdiocese of Cardiff
Tea will be served after the ceremony   at St. Joseph's High School, Tredegar Park, Newport, Mon.

Invitation to Official Opening of Phase I on 5th May 1970.

Construction Activity (Phase I): Assembly Hall (left) and House Block.

Construction Activity (Phase I): House Block (left) and Practical Block.

Rt. Hon. Edward Short, M.P., unveiling Plaque; Mr. Joseph Witherington, Headmaster.

Official Guests at Opening Ceremony – From right to left: Sister Pauline, Most Rev. Archbishop John Murphy, Rev. Mother Finbarr, Mr. John Long (Town Clerk of Newport Borough Council), the Mayor of Newport, Mrs. Lillian Bowen, the Mayoress, Rev. Luke Delaney, Rt. Hon. Edward Short, M.P., Rt. Rev. Bishop Daniel Mullins.

The School Assembly.

The Small Hall.

A classroom in the House Block.

Access Corridor.

The Main Hall.

Phase II

Although Newport Education Authority had stated that their plans envisaged an end-on project for the building of Phases I and II, hopes of achieving this were dashed when it was reported in December 1968 that Phase II had definitely been postponed, and that the earliest date for its commencement appeared to be 1973. Newport's projects at Hartridge, St. Julian's and Lliswerry Schools had replaced St. Joseph's in the building programme. This was a bitter disappointment.

The meetings and correspondence, which had dominated between 1964 and 1969, were to be repeated for Phase II in the discussions with Newport Borough and the Welsh Office. The Governors felt that it was imperative for Phase II to be included in the 1971/72 Programme in priority over other projects, and asked Newport Education Committee to receive a deputation.

Despite the subsequent meeting, the Education Authority did not put Phase II into the 1971/72 Programme. They did, however, request that the Department of Education and Science put Phase II behind projects for Lliswerry and Nash, with a proposed start on site on 1st April 1972.

Subsequently, it was proposed by the Association that a deputation be sent to the DES to seek permission for the building of Phase II. The LEA did not support this deputation. The Catholic Parents' and Electors' Association organised a public meeting and a petition of parents' signature to support this request.

In December 1970, at the instigation of the Association, a joint meeting of its officers and the Governors decided that a letter should be sent to:

- The Chief Education Officer for Newport;
- The Secretary of State for Wales asking him to meet a deputation from both the Governors and the Association.

It was agreed that the deputation should comprise: the Chairman at that time, Alderman Mrs. Mary Dunn, Bishop Daniel Mullins, Alderman Percy Jones, Alan Shewring, Tony Boyle, and Joseph Witherington, the Headmaster.

The meeting took place at the Mansion House in Newport on 8th January 1971. The Secretary of State for Wales, Peter Thomas, M.P., was accompanied by officials from the Welsh Office including his top civil servant, Mr. D. T. Marshall, and the Chief Inspector of Schools in Wales, Wyn Lloyd. This meeting proved to be crucial and had been arranged through the good offices of Roy Hughes, M.P. for Newport, and courtesy of His Worship the Mayor of Newport, Alderman Sydney Miller. The crisis facing Governors and parents was explained to the Minister, and after a good discussion, he agreed to send his Chief Inspector, Wyn Lloyd, to visit the three Schools to assess their adequacy.

The Chief Inspector's conclusions, subsequent to his inspection of the Schools, were that the Junior High Schools faced a difficult position in September 1971, and that a crisis situation was developing in the ensuing years. Mr. Gratton, his assistant, stated that the statistics of pupils transferring from the feeder Catholic primary schools revealed that the School quickly became a twelve form entry School, and that, consequently, the whole of the building programme needed to be reconsidered in the light of these facts.

A crucial factor in all this was the production of the Public Notice establishing the School in 1967, which confirmed that the catchment area as defined in that document did, in fact, include Chepstow and the districts of South Monmouthshire. This fact was seriously doubted by the Inspector until the Public Notice itself was produced at the joint meeting of the Governing Body and the Association, held in the Gilt Room in Tredegar House, to which Messrs. Lloyd and Gratton reported their findings. It is interesting how seemingly small detail can swing an argument. During the meeting, when doubt was cast on the catchment area of the School, the file containing the Public Notice was brought in to the meeting from Alan Shewring's home, proving to the Inspector the veracity of the argument. (A copy of the Public Notice is reproduced in Appendix 1.)

Wyn Lloyd then informed the representatives of the two bodies that he would report his conclusions to the Minister and the Department in Cardiff and advocate that immediate measures be taken to alleviate the crisis situation.

As a result of the meeting in the Gilt Room, Bishop Mullins, Clerk to the Governors, wrote to the Secretary of State requesting details of the results of Wyn Lloyd's inspection, and to the CEO for Newport informing him of the facts reported by Mr. Gratton concerning the size of the intake and the limits of the catchment area. A joint letter from the Governors and the Association was sent to D. T. Marshall at the Welsh Office presenting all the points that had emerged at the meeting and requesting that provision be made to avert the crisis situation that threatened.

On 4th October 1971, Bishop Mullins read out a letter from D. T. Marshall stating that £398,637 had been allocated for the construction of Phase II. It was confirmed that a start could be made before 31st March 1972. It was later affirmed by the Newport-based architects, Bates and Price, that the overall contract period was from March 1972 to September 1974, but that it should be completed within two years. The relief and satisfaction felt by all concerned at this news was palpable. The Association felt it was nearing its ultimate objective with a great sense of achievement, although there were still battles to be waged and won, notably Phase III, comprising the sixth form suite, and the playing fields.

Phase II was duly completed in 1974, and at last all pupils were housed on one site, with the two Junior High Schools being vacated. During this year, Tredegar House was sold to Newport Borough Council by the Sisters and as a result, a legal notice to vacate was served on the Governors. Temporary use of the old Canteen Building was granted for use by the sixth form pupils.

Phase III

In October 1974, it was decided that the Chairman of Governors, Alan Shewring, and Bishop Mullins should request a meeting at the Welsh Office to discuss the building of Phase III. As a result of this meeting with Miss Arnold, permission was granted by the Welsh Office to build the sixth form suite, which was completed in the summer of 1976. The meetings, correspondence and unremitting effort concerning the establishment and building of the School since 1964, had at last been brought to fruition.

During the School's construction, the access road from the A48 was built and was originally planned by Newport County Borough without a walkway or pavement for pedestrians. This set alarm bells ringing for the safety of pupils travelling to and from School. A meeting was hastily arranged with the Town Clerk, John Long, and the Chairman, together with Councillor Dick Murray, the Vice-chairman. The Town Clerk tried to re-assure us that this was the modern way in which road planning was developing. However, our concern for the safety of pupils eventually convinced him and he graciously agreed to have a walkway provided.

Again, the original plans by Newport for access and egress to the School from the above road envisaged only one entrance for buses and cars with a roundabout. Our view that there should be separate access and egress points were accepted after some discussion.

The completed School, with its superb facilities, brought justifiable pride to all concerned, and was to provide an enviable environment in which generations of pupils would be educated. The Science Laboratories, Gymnasium, Practical Block, Hall of Sport, Assembly Hall and Music Rooms were all of a very high standard and provided facilities which were greatly admired. Additionally, the setting of the School, in the grounds of Tredegar House and adjacent to the lake, which was used for canoeing instruction, was delightful. Although it would be some years before purpose-made playing fields were laid, the area between the avenue of oaks in Tredegar House grounds provided superb football, rugby and hockey pitches.

It was undoubtedly one of the finest lay-outs of its time for any comprehensive school.

Aerial View of School with Tredegar House in background.

Extract from 100 strong school staff photograph showing Headmaster and senior staff in 1977.

TIME FOR CELEBRATION

The Officers and Members of the Association felt immensely privileged to have been able to play such a large part in the founding of St. Joseph's High School. In retrospect, it is amazing how much a small group of parents achieved against all the odds in those early days. The vital part played by Sister Pauline and the Sisters of St. Joseph cannot be over-stated, for without their generosity of spirit the School would not have been based at Tredegar House. All those who were involved in the project had a great sense of pleasure and satisfaction that the means of providing a first class Catholic Secondary education for the children of Newport and South Gwent had been established. The School has gone from strength to strength and has achieved not only parity of esteem with its counterparts in the state sector but has surpassed many.

With the completion in late 2004 of the superb new School, replacing its predecessor after 37 years, a new phase is beginning in the life of St. Joseph's High School. The Head, Sue Jenkins, and the Governors, led by the Chairman, Paul Bennett, are to be congratulated on the new building situated on Pencarn Way, to the south of Tredegar House and the original School.

The original buildings were of an innovative design of two-storey grouped units, punctuated by recreational courts and inter-connected at ground and first floor levels. The height restriction was imposed by the Historic Building Council. Unfortunately, the buildings had flat roofs, a feature of 1960s structures, which eventually proved irreparable economically.

51

In writing *Birth of a School* I have tried to describe the events leading up the establishment of the School, and the subsequent building development which was finally completed in 1976 with the opening of the Sixth Form Suite. At that point, the project was substantially completed, although the negotiations in respect of the playing fields dragged on. There were also protracted negotiations with Newport Borough Council to agree the exchange of land which extended from June 1975 to March 1978. Therefore, this is not a definitive history of the School extending to the present time.

The future of St. Joseph's High School is assured as the new School buildings, with their 21st Century facilities, are now occupied. This State-of-the-Art School provides wonderful opportunities for all pupils of all abilities and disciplines. The good wishes of the whole Catholic community of Newport and South Gwent are with Sue Jenkins and her colleagues in this next exciting phase in the history of St. Joseph's R.C. High School.

Ursula O'Reilly, Head Girl (went to read Law at Wadham College, Oxford 1977), and Philip Constable, Head Boy (went to read History at Downing College, Cambridge 1977) receiving the Headmaster's Prize, Prize Day 1977.

Anthony Ray, Head Boy 1979, receiving his Welsh Rugby Cap from Mr. E. H. Loudon, Director of Education, Gwent, Prize Day 1977.

Stephen Porretta (went to read Physics at Wadham College, Oxford 1980) receiving the Monsanto Award for Science and Technology 1977, from the Headmaster.

Sian Sturdy receiving the Trophy from H. Williamson, Chairman of the White Fish Authority, as winner of the U.K. Cookery Competition 1972.

Sisters Pauline, Carmel and Madeleine Sophie with Members of the Governing Body, Headmaster and Head Boy, Anthony Mulcahy, and Head Girl, Patricia Whiting.

54

School Orchestra and Choir.

New School (November 2004).

School playing fields with Tredegar House in background.

56

APPENDIX 1

PUBLIC NOTICE OF PROPOSAL TO ESTABLISH SCHOOL

NEWPORT (MONMOUTHSHIRE) LOCAL EDUCATION AUTHORITY

NOTICE is hereby given in accordance with the provisions of Section 13(3) of the Education Act 1944 that we, the undersigned, propose to establish a new secondary school, to be maintained by the Local Education Authority for about 1,700 children, mainly of the age of 11-18 at Tredegar Park, St. Bride's Road in the County Borough of Newport (Monmouthshire). It is intended that the said school shall be conducted as an Aided Voluntary School, and religious instruction will be given in school hours in accordance with the provisions of Section 28(1) of the Act and in conformity with the doctrines of the Roman Catholic Church.

The school will be available for the following districts:

The County Borough of Newport and the following districts of Monmouthshire adjacent to the Borough boundary from which by agreement with the Monmouthshire LEA, extra districts pupils will be drawn – Bedwas and Machen Urban District, Risca Urban District, Magor and St. Mellons Rural District (West), Caerleon Urban District, Chepstow Urban District, Magor and St. Mellons Rural District (East) and Chepstow Rural District (South).

The Managers or Governors of any voluntary school affected by these proposals or any ten or more local government electors for the area for which it is proposed to establish the Schools or any local education authority concerned may submit objections to the proposals by a letter addressed to the Secretary for Welsh Education, Education Office for Wales, 31 Cathedral Road, Cardiff, which should reach him within two months after the date of the first publication of this Notice.

Signatures of Proposers: *JOHN A. MURPHY*
                                  PETER F. GAVIN
                                  JOSEPH O'CONNOR
                                  EDMUND J. MULLINS

Dated: *27th May 1967*

Section 13(2) and (3) of the Education Act 1944 as amended by Section 16 of the Education (Miscellaneous Provisions) Act 1953 provides as follows:

"(2) Where any persons propose that any school established by them or by persons whom they represent which at the time being is not a voluntary school, or any school proposed to be so established, should be maintained by a local education authority as a voluntary school, they shall after consultation with the authority submit proposals for that purpose to the Secretary of State.

(3) After any proposals have been submitted to the Secretary of State under this Section, the authority or persons by whom the proposals were submitted shall forthwith give public notice of the proposals in the prescribed

manner and the managers or governors of any voluntary school affected by the proposals or any ten or more local government electors for the area and any local education authority concerned may, within two months after the first publication of the notice submit to the Secretary of State objections to the proposals."

Explanatory Note

(This note is not part of the Notice but is intended to explain its general purport)

It is proposed to reorganise the arrangements for the provision of secondary education for Roman Catholic children who have attained the age of 11 years in the County Borough of Newport, and certain parts of Monmouthshire immediately contiguous to the Borough boundary. The proposals will enable the Roman Catholic Authorities to reorganise their arrangements for secondary education on a comprehensive basis which will fit in with the existing Newport Local Education Authority organisation for such education.

From September 1967 Roman Catholic boys and girls of 11 to 13 years living within the agreed catchment area will attend respectively, the existing Father Hill Secondary School for Boys and the existing Holy Family R.C. Secondary School for Girls, which will then become junior comprehensive schools and will be known respectively, as St. Joseph's Junior High School for Boys and St. Joseph's Junior High School for Girls. Certain teaching rooms at the existing Father Hill and Holy Family Schools will be adapted as specialist teaching accommodation for pupils of 11 to 13 years.

Roman Catholic pupils of both sexes of the ages 13 to 18 years will be accommodated in the new R.C. Senior Comprehensive School which is to be established at Tredegar Park, and which will be known as St. Joseph's High School. From September 1967 pupils of the existing Father Hill and Holy Family Schools will be transferred to the proposed St. Joseph's High School at the end of the school year in which they become 13. The school will be accommodated initially in the premises of the former St. Joseph's Independent Convent School, which will cease as from that date, supplemented by temporary hutted accommodation. This accommodation will be further supplemented by the first instalment of the permanent buildings for the new school, providing 600 places, which are expected to be ready in 1969.

As and when it becomes possible, further instalments of the new buildings will be provided to bring the accommodation of the new school to its long-term size of 1,700 pupils. When it becomes possible to accommodate all the 11 to 18 years R.C. pupils at Tredegar Park the proposed St. Joseph's Junior High Schools for Boys and Girls will be closed.

Girls living in Monmouthshire and at present attending St. Joseph's Convent High School and seek to remain there from September 1967, will be subject to the following arrangements and dependent upon availability of accommodation:

(1) Pupils expected to enter Forms V and VI may remain but the Monmouthshire Local Education Authority will not pay the travelling expenses of those who are non-Catholics;

(2) Catholic pupils resident in the Cwmbran/Pontypool and the Upper Western Valley who expected to enter Forms II, III and IV at St. Joseph's Convent High School will attend St. Alban's Roman Catholic High School, Pontypool;

(3) Catholic pupils resident in Caerleon, the Lower Western Valley, Bassaleg, Bedwas, Caldicot, Chepstow areas, who

expected to enter Forms II, III and IV at St. Joseph's Convent High School will continue to attend the proposed St. Joseph's High School.

(4) Non-Catholic pupils who expected to enter Forms II, III and IV at St. Joseph's Convent High School in September 1967 will then be transferred to an appropriate Monmouth-shire Local Education Authority secondary school.

Non-Catholic children resident in Newport at present attending St. Joseph's Convent High School will remain at the proposed St. Joseph's High School.

Fees will no longer be paid in respect of pupils attending St. Joseph's Convent High School after the end of this term.

APPENDIX 2

STAFF LIST 1968/69

St. Joseph's High School, Tredegar Park

Headmaster	J. Witherington	Religious Education
Deputy Head	Sister M. Pauline	Geography
Second Master	F. M. Batty	English and 4th Year
Director of Studies E5	Sister Mary Patrick	6th Year
	Mrs. S. Atherton	French/Library
	Mrs. A. M. Berry	Domestic Science
	Mrs. E. Bown	Latin/6th Form Tutor
	Sister M. Brigid	Domestic Science
	Sister M. Carmel	Home Economics
	Miss J. Cole	5th Year Teacher
	Mr. E. Curran	4th Year Leavers
	Mr. D. Evans	Science/House Master
	Sister M. Francis	Assistant 3rd Year Teacher/Commerce
	Mrs. M. Bailey	Mathematics/General Science
	Miss P. McCarthy	French/6th Form Tutor
	Mrs. P. Morgan	English
	Mr. P. Morgan	History
	Mrs. J. Owen	Physical Education (Girls)

	Miss C. Porter	Art
	Mr. S. E. Richards	3rd Year Teacher
	Mr. E. Richardson	Boys' Crafts
	Miss P. Robertson	Mathematics/6th Form Tutor
	Sister M. Sarto	Probationary Teachers
	Mr. J. Stokes	Physics
	Mr. Thomas	Chemistry
	Sister M. Vincent	Assistant 4th Year Teacher/ Needlework
	Mr. A. Wilding	Physical Education
Part Time Staff	Mrs. E. Bassett	French
	Mrs. E. Cohen	Spanish
	Sister Etheldreda	Religious Education
	Mrs. M. Gambarini	Home Nursing
	Mrs. Mullins	Music
	Miss E. Welch	Drama
Secondment	Sister M. Francis	Summer Term 1969
	Mr. E. Richardson	1969/70

St. Joseph's Junior High School for Girls

Headmistress	Sister M. Sophie	English
Deputy Head	Miss Thomas	English
	Miss Cobb	Science
	Mrs. C. Duggan	Physical Education
	Miss V. Howard	Art
	Mrs. Howells	Needlework
	Mrs. Langley	Domestic Science

	Miss Pritchard	Geography
	Sister Ursula	Remedial
Part Time Staff	Sister Brendan Joseph	History/Mathematics
	Sister Denise	Home Economics
	Mrs. Vaughan	French

St. Joseph's Junior High School for Boys

Headmaster	Mr. B. J. Dunn	Mathematics
Deputy Head	Mr. G. Drewett	English/2nd Year Master
	Mr. J. Davies*	History/Geography*
	Mr. J. Farley	Physical Education
	Mr. M. Fleming	Metalwork
	Mr. D. Flude	French/1st Year Master
	Dr. D. Flynn	Science
	Mr. A. Hicks	Remedial
	Miss J. Langford*	Mathematics*
	Mr. J. Wilkins	Art
Part Time Staff	Mr. I. Rees	Music

* In probationary year

STAFF APPOINTMENTS

26th March 1969

Senior High	Chris Cotton	Head of Geography
	Peter Stevenson	Head of DCT

23rd June 1969

Junior Girls	Miss I. M. Anderson	Drama
	Miss A. F. Arnold	Languages
	Mrs. N. Brown	English/Music
	Mrs. Eileen Connolley	Science
	Miss A. M. Johnson	Mathematics
	Mrs. J. M. Sullivan	Home Economics
Junior Boys	Mr. Alan Kethro	Art
	Mr. A. Phipps	Languages
	Mr. E. C. Thomas	Geography
Senior High	Sister Francis Clare	Head of Group Studies
	Miss H. J. Benton	Science
	Miss P. A. Bowen	Physical Education
	Thomas Evans	Head of Biology
	Michael Landers	Music
	Miss E. Lilygreen	Latin
	Miss M. P. O'Dwyer	English/History

30th October 1969

Senior High	M. Clayton	Classics
	Mrs. McGhee	English/History

23rd February 1970

Senior High	Mr. Dermot Flude	Head of Religious Education
	Mostyn Bennett	Head of Art
	Mr. Blundson	Head of Physics
	Maggie Witherington	Head of English
	R. Clayton	Classics
	P. Mullett	Rural Studies
	P. Fleming	Metalwork
	G. Waters	Woodwork

| **3rd November 1970** | Mrs. Pat Thomas | French |

24th May 1971	Graham Hobbs	Head of Geography
	Eric Bryant	Head of Group Studies
	Sister Ann-Teresa	Commercial Studies
	Miss J. Duckfield	English
	Mrs. Pat Jenkins	Mathematics
	Mrs. A. Palmer	Science
	Miss E. Williams	Art
	Mrs. F. Williams	English/History

2nd November 1972

	Jean Lewis	Art
Junior Boys	Mrs. Lonergan	English/Religious Education
	Mr. Watkins	Music & Drama/ Religious Education

19th June 1973

| **Senior High** | William Hoole | Head of Upper School |
| | William Glynn | Head of Religious Education |

66

	Brian McCann	Head of Year
	Miss M. Hughes	Physical Education
	Miss P. Bush	Group Studies
	John Haywood	English
	Peter Waters	Head of Physics
	Mr. P. Carlisham	Art
	Miss Teresa Lenahan	Group Studies
	S. B. Dorman	Group Studies
	Miss T. S. Quayle	Group Studies
	Miss E. E. Gimlett	Music & Drama
	Miss M. S. Protheroe	Biology
	Miss K. M. Paget	History/English
	Miss M. A. Hughes	Physical Education
	Mrs. K. Atkinson	Modern Languages
	Mrs. C. Were	Modern Languages
Junior Boys	Miss J. Hourihane	Mathematics
	Miss S. Stratt	History

June 1974

Senior High	Mike Bouchier	Second Deputy Head
	John Pugh	Head of Chemistry

May 1975

	Dr. D. Bradley	Head of Mathematics

June 1976

	John Hart	Deputy Head
	G. G. Jelley	DCT
	Mrs. C. B. Brown	French
	Mrs. M. Cookson	English
	B. S. White	English
	D. R. Jones	Group Studies
	Miss S. Stroud	Religious Education
	Miss M. C. O'Sullivan	Music